GAME SET MATCH *Champion* ARTHUR ASHE

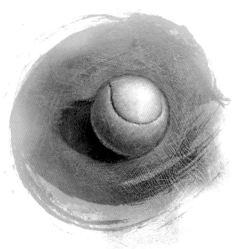

by Crystal Hubbard   illustrated by Kevin Belford

Lee & Low Books Inc.
New York

Arthur hugged his big wooden tennis racket to his chest. He was watching a young black man practicing on the Brookfield Park tennis courts in Richmond, Virginia. The man was good—as good as any of the players Arthur had seen at Byrd Park on the whites-only courts. There, Arthur could only watch from a distance as coaches instructed their students.

It was the early 1950s, and tennis facilities in Virginia were segregated, separating blacks and whites. Blacks were allowed to play at Brookfield, and for Arthur this park was home. He and his younger brother, Johnnie, lived here with their father, Daddy Ashe, the special officer in charge of the park's eighteen acres. Arthur's mother had died when Arthur was just six years old—the same age he was when he'd found the big, old wooden tennis racket and started carrying it around everywhere he went.

WHOOSH! With one smooth swing of his arm, the young black man sent a forehand shot sailing into the opposite court.

I wish I could do that, Arthur thought.

Arthur kept watching. Finally the man finished his practice and began to pack up. He had noticed Arthur too, and came over. "I can't tell if you're dragging that racket or if that racket is dragging you," the man said.

Arthur smiled shyly in response. He was used to people teasing him about being thin.

Then the man asked him a question. "Would you like to learn to play?"

"Yes, I would," Arthur said quietly.

The man Arthur had met was Ron Charity, one of the top black college tennis players in the United States. Soon Ron started giving Arthur lessons. He taught Arthur how to grip his racket; how to hit forehands and backhands, the powerful ground strokes that send the tennis ball back and forth over the net; and how to serve with speed and precision.

Arthur's arms and legs were as skinny as soda straws, but he was strong and had quick-fire reflexes. He soaked up everything Ron taught him, including the rules of the game. Arthur learned that tennis matches were divided into sets, that sets were divided into games, and that it took four points to win a game. He learned the odd scoring system that went *Love, 15, 30, 40* instead of *0, 1, 2, 3*.

Arthur was eight when he entered his first tournament at Brookfield in 1951. Playing with his heavy secondhand racket, he lost to an eleven year old. But Arthur enjoyed competing, and he continued to enter tournaments at other blacks-only parks.

Arthur started winning, and his confidence grew—a little *too* much. In a match against a child his own age who was less skilled than he was, Arthur blasted shots past his opponent. Arthur's serves were so fast, the other boy swung hopelessly at the tennis balls streaking past like comets. Every time Arthur won a point, he looked around to make sure everyone had seen it.

After the match Ron was upset.

"But I won," Arthur said, confused.

"You're supposed to play your opponent, not play up to the spectators," Ron told him. "If you ever show off like that again, I won't coach you anymore."

Arthur was ashamed. He never gloated or showed off again, not even when he beat older, stronger players and won Brookfield's annual tennis tournament. Soon Arthur was so good that Ron began taking him to the Richmond Racket Club, a private tennis club for blacks, to play against adults.

By the time Arthur was ten, he was ready for more extensive coaching. Ron and Daddy Ashe arranged for Arthur to spend summers at a tennis camp at the home of Dr. Robert Walter Johnson in Lynchburg, Virginia. Dr. Johnson was a medical doctor who loved the sport and was active in the American Tennis Association (ATA), a group formed in 1916 to allow African Americans the opportunity to play.

Dr. Johnson was also a good player. He had won several mixed doubles ATA titles with his partner and former student, Althea Gibson. Arthur knew that Dr. Johnson built champions. It was hard for Arthur to leave his family, Ron, and Brookfield; but if Ron and Daddy Ashe thought Dr. Johnson's camp was best for him, Arthur would respect their decision.

Still, Arthur had problems when he first arrived at camp. Dr. Johnson had a very different coaching style than Ron. Ron's approach was one-on-one, with Ron tossing and hitting hundreds of balls to Arthur to improve his game. Dr. Johnson had more structured training. Arthur was just one of several students there, and they used equipment to sharpen their skills.

Arthur had won lots of matches playing Ron's way. He didn't want to do anything differently. He began to act out and did not listen to Dr. Johnson. Frustrated, Dr. Johnson called Daddy Ashe, who traveled three hours to Lynchburg to talk to Arthur. Daddy Ashe was very strict, but also loving and fair. He listened to Arthur's concerns, then explained, "Ron taught you everything he could. He is the one who thought Dr. Johnson could teach you even more. Dr. Johnson is teaching you now. You do everything he says."

Arthur never defied his father. After their conversation, Arthur dedicated himself to training Dr. Johnson's way. Arthur studied Dr. Johnson's books about tennis. He sharpened his coordination using a short stick to hit a ball suspended by a string and used a special stand to practice thousands of serves. A Ball-Boy machine spat thousands of balls for Arthur to hit. He hit ground strokes against a backboard.

Dr. Johnson's neighbors complained about the *THUMPITY-BUMP* of Arthur's hard shots against the backboard at seven in the morning, but nothing could stop Arthur from practicing. Arthur realized he could hone his skills and keep winning by training Dr. Johnson's way.

During the eight years he trained with Dr. Johnson, Arthur won many titles and tournaments, competing in Virginia and other states. It didn't matter who was on the other side of the net: bigger, stronger, older, black, or white. The skinny kid with glasses unleashed blistering serves that made his opponents think their rackets had no strings. Arthur made winning look easy because he practiced so hard.

The United States began changing in the late 1950s. Segregation was being challenged in the U.S. Supreme Court, and race relations were sometimes tense. Dr. Johnson knew the only way his young black players would succeed and earn the public's respect was if they were self-disciplined and courteous. They had to be dignified always, no matter if their opponents cheated or if people called them names. Dr. Johnson taught Arthur the importance of carrying himself with calm and dignity on *and* off the court.

By Arthur's senior year of high school, Dr. Johnson and Daddy Ashe realized that Arthur would have to make another change if his skills were to improve further. Arthur needed to play tennis all year, not just in the summer. Richmond had no indoor courts for blacks, and segregation still kept Arthur off the courts for white people.

Dr. Johnson had an idea. Arthur could move to St. Louis, Missouri, to live with Richard Hudlin, a former captain of the University of Chicago tennis team. In St. Louis Arthur could play year-round. Arthur talked it over with Daddy Ashe. "I'm used to being away from home," Arthur said. "Imagine how much better my game will be if I can play all year."

Arthur was no longer a little boy, and his father respected his opinion. "I guess you're going to St. Louis," Daddy Ashe said.

In St. Louis, Arthur competed against top players. In addition to playing outdoors, he began to play indoors at places such as the 138th Infantry Armory, where he expanded his game to new court surfaces.

The armory's polished floors were slick and fast, and they helped Arthur learn to react more quickly to shots. He trained himself to hit the ball on its way up from a bounce rather than when it was coming back down. This gave his opponents less time to prepare for the return. Before, Arthur had always played from the baseline at the back of the court, relying on powerful forehand and backhand shots to send the ball over the net. The armory's faster surface forced Arthur to change his style of play. He began running up to the net after his shots to meet his opponent's returns with volleys—quick shots made before the ball can bounce. This fast, aggressive style came to be known as "serve-and-volley," and Arthur was one of the first to use it.

Arthur graduated from St. Louis's Sumner High School in 1961. He had the highest grades in his class, but it was his tennis skill that earned him a scholarship to the University of California, Los Angeles (UCLA). It was the first scholarship the school had ever given to a black tennis player.

Arthur was the twenty-eighth best amateur in America when he began at UCLA, but the school had lots of good players. Arthur was the team's number-three player behind Charlie Pasarell and Dave Reed.

As part of the college team, Arthur felt a sense of belonging. He was eager to compete against other strong teams, but Arthur quickly discovered that he still wasn't welcome to compete everywhere. The UCLA team was invited to a tournament at the Balboa Bay Club in Newport Beach, California, but the club didn't want Arthur to participate. Blacks were not allowed at Balboa Bay. Arthur's friend and teammate Charlie, a native of Puerto Rico, refused to play in support of Arthur. UCLA coach J. D. Morgan wanted to keep the whole team home, but Arthur asked him not to. Arthur thought it would be better to take such a stand at another time, when it mattered more.

Arthur didn't allow the Balboa Bay Club snub to hurt his game. In his second year at UCLA he earned a chance to play in the Championships at Wimbledon, in England. Along with the Australian, French, and United States championships, Wimbledon was a Grand Slam tennis competition, one of the sport's biggest and most respected tournaments. Winning enough matches to qualify for Wimbledon was easy for Arthur. The hard part was figuring out how to pay for the trip.

A woman named Julianna Ogner solved the problem. After watching Arthur in an exhibition match at the California Club in West Los Angeles, she approached him. "You're a remarkable player," Mrs. Ogner told Arthur. "What are your plans for the summer?"

"Playing for the Wimbledon championship, if I could get to London," Arthur said.

Mrs. Ogner offered Arthur the money he needed to make the trip. Arthur was speechless. All he could think of to say to Mrs. Ogner was "Thank you."

Mrs. Ogner was a stranger and a white woman too. Her generosity helped heal some of Arthur's pain at being excluded from Balboa Bay.

Wimbledon was a whole new world for Arthur. When he called Daddy Ashe from London, he had so much to tell him about the All England Lawn Tennis and Croquet Club. "The umpires wear hard straw hats and carnations, just as they did in 1880," Arthur said. "There's green everywhere—green ivy, green canopies, green doors and balconies and chairs."

Arthur carried his excitement to the courts. Using his serve-and-volley game, he beat his first opponent in straight sets and made it through the next round as well. In the third round Arthur faced American Chuck McKinley, the top player in the United States and an old rival from the junior circuit. Chuck was too good. He beat Arthur in straight sets and went on to win the men's singles title.

Arthur was disappointed, but he had made a good showing in his first year at Wimbledon. He had learned a lot about playing on grass courts. Grass slowed the tennis ball. The uneven surface caused the ball to make funny hops and taught Arthur to move quickly on the balls of his feet and chase down the tennis ball no matter where it bounced. Wimbledon also gave Arthur the chance to meet players from all over the world. He saw how a sport could bring people together.

Back in California at UCLA, Arthur kept competing and winning, all the while maintaining the schoolwork and grades to keep his scholarship. On August 1, 1963, he won a place on the United States Davis Cup team. The Davis Cup is the biggest international event in men's tennis, and Arthur had been a Davis Cup fan his whole life. No black man had ever been named to the American team, and Arthur was delighted to be the first. He took pride in his chance to play for his country.

In his first Davis Cup appearance at Cherry Hills Country Club near Denver, Colorado, Arthur beat Venezuela's Orlando Bracamonte in straight sets, helping the United States win the championship.

Over the next few years, Arthur continued to play and win on the college tennis circuit. His successes made his hometown of Richmond proud. On February 4, 1966, the city that had once kept him off many of its courts because of his skin color honored him by declaring Arthur Ashe Day. When Arthur spoke at the ceremony, he said, "Ten years ago this would not have happened. It is as much a tribute to Richmond and the state of Virginia as it is to me."

A few months later, Arthur graduated from college with a degree in business. He had led UCLA to the national collegiate tennis title and was the top amateur player in the United States.

The "open era" of tennis began in 1968. That meant professional players were now allowed to compete against amateurs such as Arthur. Five national tournaments were combined into one main event, the U.S. Open.

When Arthur entered the first U.S. Open championship in September he faced the best players in the world—not just the best amateurs. Arthur was completely focused, and it served him well. Match after match he advanced, beating both amateurs and professionals. After defeating South African Cliff Drysdale in a quarterfinal match and American Clark Graebner in the semifinals, Arthur was on his way to the finals.

On September 9, Arthur walked onto the court at the West Side Tennis Club in New York. This was one of the biggest matches of Arthur's life. It would not be easy, but he was ready. Arthur knew his opponent, Tom "The Flying Dutchman" Okker, well. The two had a long history of competing, and Arthur had bested Okker in their last two encounters: the quarterfinals of that year's Wimbledon tournament and the U.S. Nationals just a month before. Now The Flying Dutchman wanted revenge.

As the match began, tension was thick in the air. In the first set Arthur and Tom took no chances. The two battled game for game. Neither was able to get ahead and win by the necessary two-game lead. Arthur's powerful serve was hard for The Flying Dutchman to handle, but Tom wasn't going to give up easily. Finally Arthur served two aces—unreturnable serves—and won the first set, 14 games to 12. The Flying Dutchman battled back to win the second set, 7–5.

Relying on his big first serve, Arthur won the third set, 6–3. Tom countered by taking the fourth set, 6–3. The two men were now tied at two sets apiece. Whoever won the fifth and final set would be the champion.

With Daddy Ashe and Dr. Johnson in the stands watching, Arthur's concentration and anticipation increased. As the two players battled on, Arthur led the fifth set by two games. All he had to do was keep playing his game—serving hard, rushing the net, and placing shots out of The Flying Dutchman's reach.

Tom wanted to win as much as Arthur. Tom fought hard, using his speed and clever shot placement to win points. But Arthur was a smart player. He studied his opponents' weaknesses. Tom's was his backhand. Arthur knew better than to exploit Tom's weakness throughout the whole match; that might help his opponent strengthen his flaw. Instead, Arthur waited for just the right moment.

Arthur's patience paid off. He began hitting to Tom's backhand, and dominated the final game. With the score 40–0, Arthur only needed one more point to win.

Arthur served for the match. The sound of his racket strings striking the ball echoed like a small cannon. Then he sprang to the net to meet The Flying Dutchman's return shot and volleyed the ball out of Tom's reach.

Arthur won the final point and his first Grand Slam event. His fists clasped high in the air, Arthur stood proudly as the first U.S. Open champion. Always the good sportsman, Arthur shook Tom's hand after the match. Then he turned to see Daddy Ashe hurrying onto the court. Arthur was so happy with his victory and so proud that his father had been there to see it. Usually reserved, Arthur threw his arms around his father and hugged him right in front of everyone.

Even though Tom Okker lost the tournament, as the highest-finishing professional he received the $14,000 prize purse. Arthur, an amateur, couldn't accept anything more than a $28 a day allowance for his expenses. Arthur didn't care about the money. He wanted to keep his amateur status so he could stay eligible for Davis Cup play.

"It's nice to hear the announcer say, 'Point . . . Ashe,'" Arthur said. "But I'd rather hear him say, 'Point . . . United States.'" As much as Arthur cherished winning America's national championship, he preferred to win *for* America, in the Davis Cup competition. Three months after his U.S. Open victory, Arthur's dream came true. He and his teammates beat Australia to win the Davis Cup.

His U.S. Open and Davis Cup wins made Arthur very famous. He began playing all around the world, and he stood out everywhere he went. At twenty-five, he was the number one player in the United States and the only elite black player. Six foot one and just one hundred sixty pounds, he was so tall and skinny that people said he looked like a bow and arrow when he arched to serve a tennis ball.

In 1969, Arthur decided to become a professional. He had achieved all he could as an amateur and he wanted to earn a living as a tennis player. With little fanfare, he gave up his amateur status and began his professional career, winning the Australian Open for his second Grand Slam victory.

When Arthur went to newsstands, his own face looked back at him from the covers of *Life* and *Sports Illustrated* magazines. *The New Yorker* published a story about him. Coca-Cola and American Express wanted him to represent their products, and Head USA sporting goods created a racket called the Arthur Ashe Competition. The quiet, skinny boy from Richmond had grown into an international star.

Not comfortable just soaking up the spotlight, Arthur decided to use his fame as a tool to help other people. On a television show called *Face the Nation*, he said, "Prominent black athletes have a responsibility to champion the causes of their race." Arthur became active in getting young blacks in America interested in tennis, and he helped form a union for tennis players.

Through tennis Arthur had become a champion around the world, and he felt strongly about giving back on an international level too. Growing up with segregation in Richmond, Arthur knew how wrong and hurtful it was to be separated because of one's race. He found a cause fighting apartheid, South Africa's official policy of keeping black and white people apart.

Over and over South Africa denied Arthur entry into the country to play tennis, but Arthur kept trying. He won the support of U.S. Secretary of State William Rogers, the United States National Lawn Tennis Association, the South African Lawn Tennis Union, and South African players such as Cliff Drysdale. With help from people around the globe, Arthur got South Africa expelled from the Davis Cup competition in 1970. He brought worldwide attention to South Africa's unfair apartheid policies.

In 1973, South Africa relented and allowed Arthur to play in the South African Open. He won the men's doubles title playing with his former opponent Tom Okker. Arthur was proud that his name—a black man's name—would join a list of champions in South Africa.

By 1975, Arthur's international ranking had slipped to number five. People began to wonder if championing causes off the court had made Arthur less of a champion on it. Ever quiet and dignified, Arthur didn't talk to the newspapers or go on television shows to defend himself. He decided to tell the critics he was still a strong competitor in his own way—on the courts, at Wimbledon.

Arthur was not favored to win the tournament. He was thirty-one, passed peak age in the sport, and the previous year he had lost early in the third round. He would have to triumph over younger, stronger players such as Sweden's Björn Borg. But just as he had when he was younger, Arthur practiced hard and kept his focus on the game. One by one, round by round, he defeated the younger players, including Borg. Focused and determined, Arthur made it to the finals. There he would face his toughest rival—American Jimmy Connors.

Twenty-two year old Jimmy was the number one player in the world and the defending Wimbledon champ. The lefty had bested Arthur three times before, and Arthur knew skill alone wouldn't be enough to overcome the younger man's speed and power.

Arthur studied Jimmy's game just as he had studied his opponents in the past. Jimmy had beaten Arthur in the men's finals of the 1973 South African Open, the tournament Arthur had fought so hard to enter. Before that match Arthur had written about Jimmy in his journal. "My best strokes go to his weaknesses. My backhand is stronger than his forehand, so I'll play him down the line a lot, or right down the middle and refuse to give him the angles he likes. Also, because he likes to work with speed, I'll try to vary the pace on my shots. I expect to attack him on my second serve and lob him because his overhead is lacking."

Even though Arthur lost the match to Jimmy in 1973, Jimmy's weak spots were still the same. Arthur simply needed to hone his game plan. Leading up to the Wimbledon men's final, Arthur paid close attention to Jimmy's matches against Mexican Raul Ramirez and American Roscoe Tanner in the quarterfinal and semifinal rounds.

Ramirez tried to outwit Connors but seemed to switch strategies partway through the match. *He had the right idea but he changed his game*, Arthur thought. Tanner was a dynamic player who tried to use his power against Jimmy. "Watching Roscoe told me how not to play against [Conners]," Arthur said. "I knew that I had to be restrained in my game."

Arthur decided to use his intellect as much as his body on the court. Instead of trying to outrun, outhit, and outpower Jimmy, Arthur resolved to make Jimmy beat *himself*.

The match between Arthur and Jimmy was also personal. Opposites in almost everything, the two were adversaries off the court too. Arthur was calm and dignified. Jimmy was loud and brash. Arthur avoided the limelight and playing to the crowd. Jimmy loved attention and making a scene. Arthur was a team player. Jimmy was a one-man show. Worst of all in Arthur's mind was that Jimmy, as an amateur, had refused to play for the United States in the Davis Cup. Arthur said that decision "seemed unpatriotic." Furious, Jimmy had sued Arthur for millions of dollars.

As the Wimbledon final approached, each man prepared for the upcoming clash true to form. Arthur kept calm. He practiced and reviewed the strategy he would use against Jimmy. Jimmy made light of the match, practicing halfheartedly and joking with other players about Arthur's game.

On Saturday, July 5, 1975, Arthur and Jimmy took the Centre Court. From the start, Arthur exasperated Jimmy with serves that hooked just out of reach. Arthur raced to the net to return Jimmy's rocket-fast ground strokes, using a deft touch with volleys to soften their speed and rob them of their power.

Arthur kept the ball low when Jimmy preferred it high. He hit the ball gently over the net, forcing Jimmy to burn his own strength and energy racing to meet it. Arthur won the first set, 6–1, in nineteen minutes. He won the second set, 6–1, almost as quickly.

As the match went on, hotheaded Jimmy became more and more flustered. Sweat flew from the hair fringing his face. His cheeks turned bright red. He yelled curses and angrily threw his towel under the umpire's chair.

Jimmy's antics didn't bother Arthur. During changeovers, when the players switched sides of the court, Arthur would sit for a minute with his eyes closed and relax. Just as Dr. Johnson had taught him, Arthur remained calm and focused, never losing his cool.

Arthur's wits and grace countered Jimmy's raw, instinctive power. Jimmy attacked each shot wildly, looking so ferocious that it seemed as if he might hurl his racket. He even shouted at the crowd. But after losing two sets in a row, Jimmy battled back in the third, rallying to win the set.

When Jimmy took the lead in the fourth set, Arthur got a little nervous. He wondered if his plan was backfiring. Still, Arthur decided to stick with it and keep giving Jimmy short returns and angled volleys to tire him out. The two champions battled, but only one could win. Would it be the loud kid or the old bow and arrow?

Steadily Arthur regained control of the fourth set. Only one point stood between him and the championship, and it was his serve. Arthur was older, and not as strong as Jimmy, but his serve still had the power to intimidate. Arthur tossed the ball high. He drew back his racket arm and released it fast in a hard, sharp snap.

Jimmy lunged. His two-handed return flew back over the net. But there, waiting for it, was Arthur. He delivered a sweeping overhead smash, blasting the ball far out of Jimmy's reach.

Arthur won!

He was the first African American man to win Wimbledon. He had also claimed the number one world ranking, and he had done it by playing one of the cleverest and most exhilarating tennis matches ever.

After the match, Arthur calmly shook Jimmy's hand. Then he toweled off his face and slipped into the Davis Cup jacket he had worn to the court. As the crowd roared wildly, Arthur raised his arms to greet them, allowing a small smile to grace his face. With his own quiet strength, Arthur had proven he was still a powerful force.

1 *Shaking hands with opponents after Eastern Junior Tennis Championships doubles match, 1959* **2** *In "bow and arrow" serving form at National Tennis Championship, 1965* **3** *With Daddy Ashe after emotiona win at the inaugural U.S. Open Championship, 1968* **4** *Celebrating U.S. Davis Cup team win over France with players including John McEnroe (to the right of Ashe), 1982* **5** *Being arrested after protesting aparthei outside the South African Embassy in Washington, D.C., 1985*

AFTERWORD

In the years following his Wimbledon win, Arthur Ashe's competitive tennis career began to wind down. He became more devoted to his life off the court, and on February 20, 1977, he married a beautiful photographer named Jeanne Marie Moutoussamy. On December 12, 1986, they welcomed a daughter, naming her Camera Elizabeth.

In 1979, at the age of thirty-six, Arthur had a heart attack following a tennis clinic in New York City. Surgery fixed the problem, but his competition days were over. Being named captain of the U.S. Davis Cup tennis team eased Arthur's move off the courts. He led his team to victories in 1981 and 1982. After he stopped coaching in 1984, he became a tennis commentator for ABC and HBO and co-chairperson of the Player Development Committee of the United States Tennis Association (USTA), the organization he helped create in 1968 to promote inner-city junior players. Arthur also wrote *A Hard Road to Glory*, a three-book history of African American athletes.

Arthur's health continued to trouble him. He went to the hospital one day in 1988 after experiencing numbness in his right hand. After many tests, he found that he had HIV, the virus that causes AIDS. Doctors believed the infection came from a blood transfusion Arthur had received during a second heart surgery. Arthur had overcome chicken pox, measles, mumps, whooping cough, and diphtheria as a child. He knew that he wouldn't overcome HIV/AIDS, but he refused to let his illness break his spirit or stop him from pursuing the causes he promoted. He said, "If I were to say, 'God, why me?' about the bad things, then I should have said, 'God, why me?' about the good things that happened in my life."

Arthur joined other famous African Americans on a trip to South Africa in 1991 to witness the ending of apartheid. And in 1992, he became a champion for AIDS patients. That same year, *USA Today* told him they planned to run a story announcing he had HIV/AIDS. Arthur thought his health issues should be his own private business. Not wanting his daughter to find out he was sick from a newspaper article, he decided to reveal his illness to the world in his own way. On April 8, Arthur stood before reporters and television cameras and said, "Some of you heard that I had tested positive for HIV, the virus that causes AIDS. That is indeed the case."

People from all walks of life praised Arthur's courage. He was grateful for their compassion, and he kept fighting to raise research funds and awareness for HIV/AIDS. Arthur spoke to world leaders at the United Nations. He asked them to spend more money on AIDS education and finding a cure. He wanted to make sure people knew enough about the disease to keep from getting it and to stop being afraid of people who had it.

Arthur continued to champion other causes as well. On September 9, 1992, twenty-four years to the day after his historic U.S. Open victory, Arthur was arrested outside the White House for protesting America's poor treatment of Haitian refugees. *Sports Illustrated* named Arthur its "Sportsman of the Year" in its December 1992 issue.

Two months later, on February 6, 1993, Arthur Robert Ashe, Jr. died of AIDS-related pneumonia. He was forty-nine years old. Thousands of people lined up to say good-bye to him at the Governor's Mansion in Richmond, Virginia. More than five thousand people attended his funeral.

Even after his death Arthur continued to be a pioneer for integration. On July 10, 1996, a statue of Arthur was dedicated on Monument Avenue in Richmond. Amid white Confederate war heroes bearing sabers and sidearms stands the figure of Arthur Ashe, surrounded by children, raising books in his left hand and a tennis racket in his right hand. The inscription on the monument reads:

ARTHUR R. ASHE, JR.
1943–1993

WORLD CHAMPION, AUTHOR, HUMANITARIAN,

FOUNDER OF VIRGINIA HEROES INCORPORATED

NATIVE OF RICHMOND, VIRGINIA

THIS MONUMENT WAS PLACED AT MONUMENT AVENUE AND ROSENEATH ROAD ON JULY 10, 1996 TO INSPIRE CHILDREN AND PEOPLE OF ALL NATIONALITIES

CHRONOLOGY

1943 —July 10: Arthur Robert Ashe, Jr. born, Richmond, Virginia

1947 —Moved with family to Brookfield Park, Richmond, Virginia

1949 —Began to play tennis

1950 —Mother, Mattie Cunningham Ashe, died

1951 —Won his first match, Brookfield Park, Richmond, Virginia

1953 —First attended Dr. Walter Robert Johnson's summer tennis camp, Lynchburg, Virginia

1957 —Became first African American to play in Maryland boys' championships

1959 —Competed in first U.S. National Championships

1960 —Featured in *Sports Illustrated*'s "Faces in the Crowd"
—Earned spot on U.S. Junior Davis Cup team

1961 —Graduated from Sumner High School, St. Louis, Missouri
—Accepted college scholarship to University of California, Los Angeles

1963 —Competed in his first Wimbledon
—Became first African American man to play on U.S. Davis Cup team
—Featured again in *Sports Illustrated*'s "Faces in the Crowd"

1964 —Won Eastern Grass Court Championships, first significant win on grass courts
—Received Johnston Award for excellent play and sportsmanship

1965 —Won NCAA singles and doubles titles; team win for UCLA

1966 —February 4: Honored with Arthur Ashe Day, Richmond, Virginia
—Graduated from UCLA
—Began two-year service in U.S. Army; made assistant tennis coach at West Point

1967 —Published autobiography *Advantage Ashe*

1968 —Won U.S. Nationals and U.S. Open men's singles titles; became top-ranked amateur tennis player in the United States
—Ended two-year Army service as Second Lieutenant
—Helped the United States to Davis Cup championship
—Cofounded United States Tennis Association (USTA) National Junior Tennis League

1969 —Helped found International Tennis Players Association (later known as Association of Tennis Professionals)
—Gave up amateur status to turn professional

1970 —Launched movement to expel South Africa from Davis Cup competition because of apartheid policy
—Named a U.S. goodwill ambassador to Africa
—Won Australian Open

1973 —Granted visa to South Africa
—Became first black man to play in South African Open

1975 —Won World Championship Tennis tournament and Wimbledon; became top-ranked tennis player in the world
—Published memoir *Arthur Ashe: Portrait in Motion*

1977 —February 20: Married professional photographer Jeanne Marie Moutoussamy

1978 —Won Pacific Southwest Championships, final tournament of career

1979 —Had heart attack and open-heart surgery

1980 —Announced retirement from competition

1981 —Accepted captaincy of U.S. Davis Cup team, which went on to win championship
—Named national chairman of the American Heart Association
—Published *Off the Court*, an autobiography focusing on his life outside of tennis

1982 —Won consecutive Davis Cup championship as captain

1983 —Received blood transfusion during second heart surgery

1985 —Inducted into International Tennis Hall of Fame in Newport, Rhode Island

1986 —December 21: Daughter, Camera Elizabeth, born

1988 —Published *A Hard Road to Glory: A History of the African American Athlete*; won Emmy Award for cowriting television adaptation
—Hospitalized for numbness in right hand
—Tested positive for HIV

1992 —Announced HIV-positive status during press conference
—Arrested outside White House protesting United States policy toward Haitian refugees
—Appealed to United Nations General Assembly for funding for AIDS research and public awareness
—Named *Sports Illustrated*'s "Sportsman of the Year"

1993 —February 6: Died of AIDS-related pneumonia in New York at age forty-nine
—Funeral attended by more than five thousand, Richmond, Virginia,
—$500,000 raised by the Arthur Ashe Foundation for the Defeat of AIDS
—Memoir *Days of Grace* published
—Awarded Presidential Medal of Freedom by President Bill Clinton

1996 —July 10: Statue of Arthur Ashe dedicated, Monument Avenue, Richmond, Virginia

1997 —The U.S. Tennis Association announced new U.S. Open stadium, Arthur Ashe Stadium, National Tennis Center, Flushing, New York

2005 —U.S. Postal Service released commemorative Arthur Ashe stamp

AUTHOR'S NOTE

WHEN my oldest sister, Kim, was twelve she had a crush on Arthur Ashe, which is why I found myself in Mr. Ashe's presence not once but twice when I was eight years old. The first time, Kim wanted to attend an exhibition and clinic Mr. Ashe was conducting at the 178th Artillery Armory in St. Louis. Our mother dropped us off, and Kim was to supervise my sisters and me. But Kim didn't pay us any attention. She only had eyes for Mr. Ashe. Maybe she thought they were destined for each other, since he and our mother shared a July 10 birthday. Whatever his appeal, I didn't see it. He was taller and skinnier than any man I knew. Still, when Mr. Ashe spoke, his quiet, even voice managed to calm everyone in the arena, even me, a practiced jabber mouth.

When Mr. Ashe sat to sign autographs after the clinic, Kim was so shy and love-struck that she froze. Her tense, sweaty hands shoving my shoulders were the last thing I felt before I found myself standing before Mr. Ashe. He took a black-and-white 8 x 10 photo of himself from a pile at his elbow.

"What's your name?" he asked in that alarmingly calm voice.

"Crystal," I told him. Mr. Ashe began writing on the photo.

"Could you make it out to Kim too?" I asked.

"Of course," Mr. Ashe said.

"And Kelly?" I asked. "And Joelle. And Lauren too."

Mr. Ashe smiled as he uncapped his pen again. "Who are all these people?"

"My sisters," I told him. "They're over there." I pointed to a column behind which Kim was partially hidden. Even from halfway across the room I could see the flame-red tips of her ears.

Mr. Ashe raised a hand and waved. Kim disappeared behind the column.

I thanked him for the photo and started away, but he called after me. Perhaps he'd noticed that my sisters and I were, along with him, among the very few people of color in attendance. "Do you and your sisters play tennis?" he asked.

"I don't," I told him. "But my sister Kim does."

"Good," Mr. Ashe said. "That's very good."

As I handed the photo over to Kim, I couldn't stop thinking about Mr. Ashe. He was dressed like a tennis player, and I'd just seen him play, but I couldn't stop thinking of him as a teacher. His bright smile, distinctive glasses, and instructive yet warm delivery added up to a science teacher in my eight-year-old brain, not a superstar athlete.

Once we got home and Mr. Ashe's photo disappeared under Kim's pillow, I didn't think of him again until the next autograph signing Kim dragged us to, at a department store. Again I was the designated autograph retriever, and again my sisters and I were among the few people of color at the event. Things went a bit differently when I approached Mr. Ashe this time.

"Crystal, isn't it?" he said.

I felt famous. I couldn't open my mouth to speak. So I nodded. Mr. Ashe took a photo from his neat stack and began writing my name on it. Without looking up, he said, "Where's she hiding this time?"

"Who?" I said stupidly.

"Kim."

"Over by the water fountain," I said.

Mr. Ashe waved at Kim, finished writing, and shook my hand. "Good to see you again."

"My mother made us take tennis lessons at Tower Grove Park," I reported.

"Did you like it?" he asked.

"No," I admitted honestly. "But I like hitting the balls against the garage."

"That's a start," Mr. Ashe said, and laughed.

Our paths never crossed again after that afternoon. I eventually developed a love of tennis that, like Dr. Walter Robert Johnson, led me to pursue instruction in the game in my mid-twenties. On public courts I would envision myself in pristine whites, kneeling before the Royal Box on Centre Court before becoming the oldest player ever to win the women's singles title at Wimbledon.

In 1993, when Mr. Ashe died of AIDS-related pneumonia, I had a moment of appreciation for him that I'd never experienced before. I thought about the last time I'd sought his autograph and what he'd written on his photo. He'd remembered my name. And he'd remembered Kim's too. But he'd also remembered Kelly, Joelle, and Lauren, and he'd put their names on the photo without any prompting from me. Mr. Ashe, a man who had conquered a sport typically closed to people of color, who had walked with dignitaries and seen the world, remembered a little girl with pigtails who didn't like to play tennis.

Arthur Robert Ashe, Jr. is remembered as a champion, a man who became a citizen of the world and who had a vast impact not only on sports but on the way people treat one another. I'll always remember him as a man who made a lasting impression on a quirky little tomboy with a passion for writing. *Days of Grace*, Mr. Ashe's final memoir, ends with words to his daughter. Given his generosity and kindness, I remain convinced that these words are a gift to us all: "[W]herever I am when you feel sick at heart and weary of life, or when you stumble and fall and don't know if you can get up again, think of me. I will be watching and smiling and cheering you on."

AUTHOR'S SOURCES

BOOKS

Ashe, Arthur, and Arnold Rampersad. *Days of Grace*. New York: Ballantine Books, 1994.

Ashe, Arthur, and Frank Deford. *Arthur Ashe: Portrait in Motion*. New York: Carroll & Graf Publishers, 1993.

Mantell, Paul. *Arthur Ashe: Young Tennis Champion (Childhood of Famous Americans)*. New York: Aladdin, 2006.

Steins, Richard. *Arthur Ashe: A Biography*. Santa Barbara: Greenwood Press, 2005.

Towle, Mike. *I Remember Arthur Ashe: Memories of a True Tennis Pioneer and Champion of Social Causes by the People Who Knew Him*. Nashville: Cumberland House Publishing, 2001.

PERIODICALS

Deford, Frank. "Service, But First a Smile." *Sports Illustrated*, August 29, 1966.

———. "The Once and Future Diplomat." *Sports Illustrated*, March 1, 1971.

Gray, David. "Arthur Ashe's blow for peace." *Manchester Guardian*, July 5, 1975.

Moore, Kenny. "Sportsman of the Year." *Sports Illustrated*, December 21, 1992.

———. "He Did All He Could." *Sports Illustrated*, February 15, 1993.

Price, S. L. "Slow Train to Eminence." *Sports Illustrated 40th Anniversary Issue*, September 19, 1994.